DATE DUE ☑ **W9-ASL-389**

Oranges to Orange Juice

By Inez Snyder

Welcome Books™

Children's Press®
A Division of Scholastic Inc.
New York / Toronto / London / Auckland / Sydney
Mexico City / New Delhi / Hong Kong
Danbury, Connecticut

Photo Credits: Cover and all photos by Maura B. McConnell
Contributing Editor: Jennifer Silate
Book Design: Mindy Liu

Library of Congress Cataloging-in-Publication Data

Snyder, Inez.
   Oranges to orange juice / by Inez Snyder.
   p. cm. — (How things are made)
   Includes index.
   ISBN 0-516-24265-2 (lib. bdg.) — ISBN 0-516-24357-8 (pbk.)
   1. Orange juice. I. Title. II. Series.

TX558.O7 S64 2003
641.8'75—dc21

                                        2002007168

Contents

My name is Meena.

Today, Dad and I are making **orange juice** from oranges.

5

First, Dad has to cut the oranges.

He **carefully** cuts each orange in **half**.

This is a **juicer**.

It is used to **squeeze** juice from the oranges.

9

I put half of an orange
in the juicer.

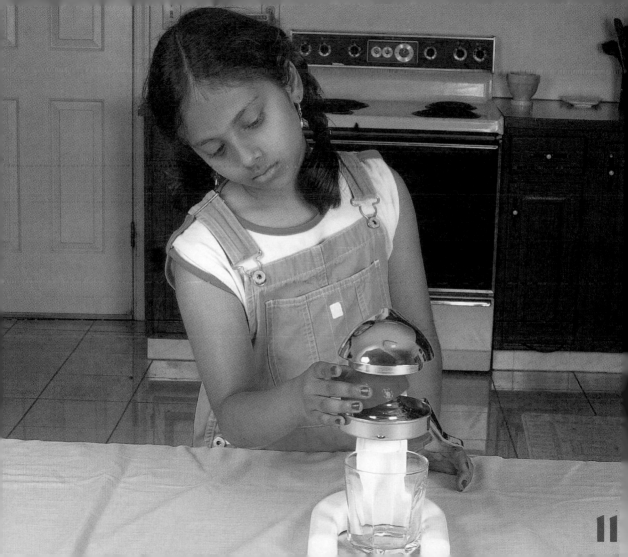

Dad pushes on the juicer's **handle**.

The top part of the juicer presses down on the orange.

13

Look!

The orange juice is going into my glass.

The glass is not full yet.

We have to make more orange juice.

I put another half of
an orange in the juicer.

Dad lets me push down
on the handle.

I push down hard.

19

Now, my glass is full.

The orange juice is good!

New Words

carefully (**kair**-fuhl-ee) paying close attention

half (**haf**) one of two equal parts of something

handle (**han**-duhl) the part of an object that is used to carry, move, or hold that object

juicer (**joos**-uhr) a machine that gets liquid from fruits and vegetables

orange juice (**or**-inj **joos**) liquid that comes from an orange

squeeze (**skweez**) to press something firmly together from opposite sides

To Find Out More

Books
Orange Juice
by Betsey Chessen and Pamela Chanko
Scholastic Trade

Oranges
by Claire Llewellyn
Children's Press

Web Site
Florida Citrus Land
http://www.floridajuice.com/floridacitrus/kids
This Web site has fun games, recipes, and lots of information about orange juice.

Index

About the Author
Inez Snyder writes and edits children's books. She also enjoys painting and cooking for her family.

Reading Consultants
Kris Flynn, Coordinator, Small School District Literacy, The San Diego County Office of Education

Shelly Forys, Certified Reading Recovery Specialist, W.J. Zahnow Elementary School, Waterloo, IL

Sue McAdams, Former President of the North Texas Reading Council of the IRA, and Early Literacy Consultant, Dallas, TX